GIVING FACE:

The Art to Looking Flawless for Every Occasion

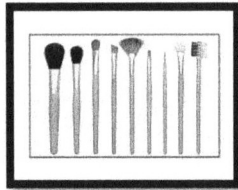

GIVING FACE:

The Art to Looking Flawless for Every Occasion

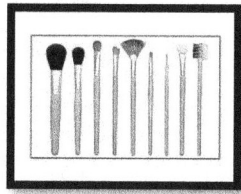

Courtney Rashon

Cosby Media Productions ™

Entertaining the Mind, and Inspiring the Soul

Published by Cosby Media Productions

www.cosbymediaproductions.com

Cover art: Cosby Media Productions

Edited by: Tamar Hela

ISBN-13: 978-0692742372

ISBN-10: 0692742379

WHAT OTHERS ARE SAYING

"It's always pleasure collaborating with Courtney. Her creativity, and ideas always brings a lil' more to the projects we work on together. On top of that, she has a knack for dealing with actors. Her personality is like a calming filter before all the talent arrives on set to shoot a scene. Dealing with various types of personalities as a director . . . that goes a long way."

Paul Coy Allen – Director

It's an absolute pleasure and a total delight to work with Courtney Rashon. Her attention to detail in terms of her clients' needs are impeccable, and the professionalism that she displays is second to none. The comfort I felt with her stylistic insight were as valuable as they were a necessity, and I would recommend her services to anyone serious about their image in any capacity in the entertainment business.

Jopaul – Recording Artist

There is a saying that the universe gives you everything that you need. What's The 411TV was in need of a beauty correspondent and in walked Courtney Rashon! We received more than a beauty correspondent; Courtney Rashon is a beauty expert, skillful, key makeup artist, and an entertainment maven. It is a real joy to work with her.

Ruth Morrison – Television Producer – What's the 411TV

TABLE OF CONTENTS

DEDICATION

This book is dedicated to:

My Heavenly Creator, God Almighty. Thank you for giving me life, love, and wisdom. Without You, nothing is possible.

To my mother, who exposed me to the world of beauty and my grandmothers who are the family matriarchs of style, elegance, and fabulousness.

To all of my best friends for their unique looks, gorgeous features, and individuality.

Cheryl, for her minimalistic makeup and beautiful blue eyes. Sarah, for her perfect caramel skin. Roya, for her exotic features and her perfectly arched eyebrows. Loreal, for embracing her freckles and her fresh-faced, glowing skin. Kuandika, for always wearing a ruby red on her bow shaped full lips, no matter what the occasion is. Melissa, for keeping her face beat and her exaggerated luxurious eyelashes on fleek. And my cousin, Tosha, for schooling me that petroleum jelly is one of the best moisturizers on the planet, which is how she keeps her cocoa brown skin shiny and supple all those years.

To all the women in my family, who have always embodied generations and future generations of women who always look their best on every occasion! Thank you all for inspiring me. I love you all to pieces!

I also want to thank my family for always supporting me in everything that I do. Without them, I would not have the strength to pursue each and every endeavor that I wanted. To my brothers, who have always made sure I kept a manicure and pedicure and would make fun of me if I did not. That taught me the importance of being well-groomed as a woman and informing me of all the things that we don't think guys pay attention to.

Finally, my biggest inspiration is my son. At the end of the day, I do it all for him.

INTRODUCTION

My inspiration for becoming a makeup artist was my mother, Sharon Sims-Mosley, who is an extremely talented licensed cosmetologist. Her niche and reputation for "having a green thumb" when it comes to hair care, maintenance, and styling was her M.O. among her peers and clients. Every day after school, I was her "shampoo girl," and I witnessed firsthand the beauty rituals that women were addicted to.

Watching my mother transform her clients through her impressive work with hair and makeup always amazed me. I attended beauty trade shows with her while she was working on a platform, competing in a competition, or just attending the event. I even sometimes attended classes on hair color and makeup, and volunteered to be a model and have my hair cut and styled by prominent stylists from all over the state. Since my mother was the hair guru, my cousins and I always had the latest haircuts, colors, and makeup before the trends even came out. She is *that* amazing!

All of this taught me the importance of looking and feeling your best. Confidence is something that all people— especially women—struggle with. Makeup and hair styling should not be the reason for confidence, but it damn sure makes you feel good when your face is beat and your hair is flowing.

Creativity was always in my blood and I was yearning to bleed. In high school, I was constantly the one adding a dab of blush, eyeliner, and mascara to my friends and myself as well. After I attended college in New Jersey, I worked in the music industry and also in fashion. In between jobs, I decided to follow my passion and pursue makeup. I enrolled in a beauty school that offered an intense makeup program in New York to learn the art, science, and fundamentals of makeup. The makeup program consisted of three courses: Fashion/Glamour, Character Sciences, and Visual F/X. I earned my certificates and received praise from my instructors on my skills and creativity . . . and the rest is history!

I have been blessed to work with some talented and amazing people. It was a pleasure to bring their vision to life while incorporating my own creative spin into the look. The results were perfect. I sincerely thank all of them for allowing me such great opportunities and believing in my skills.

The concept of the book is based on having a relationship with your makeup. By learning to embrace and understand your facial features with creativity, you will be able to transform yourself into a beautiful you who looks her best for every occasion. Learn to fall in love with makeup.

CHAPTER 1: EYES ARE THE WINDOW TO THE SOUL

Eyes and eyebrows are intricate parts of your face. Many people do not realize that a message can be sent without speaking, but by only using your eyes and eyebrows. Eyebrows are key features of the face. The eyes tell a story that can be interpreted without words. When using your eyes as a form of communication, make sure your eyebrows always look fabulous!

Eyebrows frame your face. Whether natural or enhanced, eyebrows should always be neat and not extend much farther beyond the outer corners of your eyes with a natural arch. The inner ends or corners of the eyebrows should be aligned with the crease of the nostril, regardless of how full your eyebrows are.

Adding lash-like strokes in between hairs is a great way to fill in your eyebrows. Filling in eyebrows can be done with powder or pencil to achieve this perfect look. After this is done, brush the eyebrows out to blend in the pencil and eyebrow filler with the entire brow. If shadow or powder is used, then this step is not necessary. For natural brows, a brow gel can be used to tame unruly eyebrow hairs and keep them neat.

There are various techniques to achieve the perfect eyebrow. Waxing and threading are very popular eyebrow grooming techniques. Plucking eyebrows are ideal for touch-ups in between grow-outs. But over-plucking can cause your eyebrows to look uneven in some cases. Plucking should be done in-between waxing and threading, unless you have mastered the art of eyebrow plucking and can do it yourself to maintain eyebrow grooming.

The eyebrows set the stage of someone's face. Women must understand that the perfect arch is not impossible. There are many options for natural eyebrows that involving sculpting and shaping. To achieve a perfect arch, you should first allow your eyebrows to grow out as much as they can. There are many options, including tattooing, tweezing, threading, and waxing. All of these techniques are great, but can be hazardous and hideous if done incorrectly. Here are some tips for each technique, as well as advice on eyebrow maintenance:

Tattooing should be done only if the hairs on your eyebrows do not fully grow in. Also, this would be ideal for someone who does not have the time to always use a pencil or shadow. The look should be natural, and the artist should follow the natural shape of your eyebrow.

Tweezing is great for touchups in between eyebrow maintenance. Be careful not to pluck too much because this can lead to redness and irritation. Always make sure that your tweezers are sanitized and have a sharp point. I recommend using an eyebrow kit. These kits contain all the essentials for fierce eyebrows.

Threading The threading technique is a traditional method some cultures have always used to groom their eyebrows. It involves using thread instead of wax to remove the hairs from your eyebrows. I personally prefer this technique if you have full eyebrows. It lasts longer than traditional waxing and is usually less expensive. If done properly your eyebrows will look amazing!

Waxing is the most popular way of controlling eyebrows.

The technician should be careful not to "chop" the end or the "tail" of your eyebrow off. I would recommend that the brow technician start first by combing the hairs on the eyebrow upward and then trim them with scissors. Next, apply the wax to the top of the eyebrow and underneath and follow the natural arch. Tweezing can be done for stray hairs instead of reapplying wax to the eyebrow repeatedly. This can cause the eyebrows to get thinner and change their natural shape. Remember to always wax between the eyebrows to avoid a uni-brow Have the technician follow up with aloe vera or an after-waxing coolant gel to prevent inflammation. Make sure the technician uses a new wax strip or "waxing stick" before the wax is applied to your eyebrows. Being sanitary and clean is protocol and mandatory by the State Board Laws of Cosmetology for any beauty salons or spas located in the U.S.

The shape of your eyes determines how your eye makeup should be applied. I've listed the basic eye shapes and the makeup techniques that should be used to achieve your best look for any occasion.

For **almond eyes**, the best technique to enhance the eyes for a defined look would be to increase the depth and intensity. This entails applying lighter matte shades from the corner of your eyes until the end of the brow bone. A sweep of a lighter shimmer should be applied across the entire lid. To make the eyes appear larger, tightly line the upper eyelash line with a dark matte shade only. Almond eyes are perfectly symmetrical and have the most versatility for any look because of their shape.

For **round eyes**, a medium color should be applied to the eyelid first. Afterwards, sweep a lighter matte shade across the eyebrow bone. This will highlight the eyes immensely. Tightly line the outer corners of the upper eyelash line with a darker shade to draw attention to the outer corners of your eyes. By doing this, your eyes will appear more defined, as well as elongated, which will maximize the shape.

For **deep-set eyes**, a highlighter shade should be applied along the inner corner of the lower eyelash line and the eyebrow bone. Next, apply a medium or mid-tone shade up and above the crease of the eyes and sweep the color across the entire lid until where the eyebrow bone ends. Then, apply the accent shade to the outer corners of the upper eyelash line and extend onto the corner of the eyebrow bone. Sweep the accent shade underneath the lower eyelash line for maximum definition. Blend all three shades together until they harmonize.

When lining your eyes, draw a very thin line of eyeliner along the upper and lower eyelash line and thicken the line slightly outwards. Use an eyebrow or eyeliner brush to soften the edges. Apply several coats of mascara as always.

For **eyes that are spaced apart** or **wide-set**, first apply a light or neutral shade to the entire lids of the eyes. Extend the shade slightly to the outer corners of the eyes and a tad bit above the crease of the eyes. Then, apply a thin line of color right below the eyes. It should be the same color or very close to the color on the eyelids. Using a darker shade, like deep dark brown, apply the color towards the inner corners of the eyes and blend it towards the outer corners. This will make the eyes appear narrower because of the color in the inner corners. Highlight the eyebrow bone using a lighter shimmer shade towards the center, directing the color along the eyes to the pupils. Blend well into the crease of the color. Add a very dark shade and tap it into the corners of the eyes while extending it to the middle of the eyes for the illusion of closer eyes. Apply mascara. This technique will have your eyes looking fab!

For **eyes that are upturned**, the trick is to emphasize and create an upward lift in appearance and enhance the symmetry. Upturned eyes are the perfect shape for a smoky-eyed look. First, apply a lighter matte shade to the eyebrow bone, and then sweep a light shimmer shade across the entire lids. Thinly line the upper eyelash line with a darker shade. Then, using the same shade, draw a thicker line at the outer corners of the lower eyelash line to enhance symmetry to complete the look. Once again, apply mascara!

For **eyes that are downturned**, the shape of the eye should be accentuated and enhanced on the outer corners. Sweep a lighter shimmer shade across the entire eyelid. Apply a matte shade directly underneath the eyebrow bone. Add a thin line to the entire upper eyelash line with a darker shade, extending outward and upward to create a "cat eye." Make sure not to line the lower eyelash line. This eye shape is perfect for creating the "cat eye" look. Always use mascara.

For creating dimension with **monolid eyes,** a light shade should be swept right underneath the eyebrow bone. Apply a medium shade to the entire lids of the eyes. Line both the upper and lower eyelash lines with a darker matte shade with a thinner line at the lower eyelash line. Apply several coats of mascara to complete this look. This will give the appearance of more definition instantly!

Hooded eyes require a lighter shade underneath the entire the eyebrow bone. Then, sweep a medium matte shade across the entire lids of the eyes. To create the appearance of larger eyes, simply draw a thin line on the upper eyelash line using a dark matte shade. Mascara should be applied after the application is completed. The eyes will appear much bigger and brighter!

SMOKY EYE TECHNIQUE

One of the most popular techniques and timeless looks of eye makeup is the smoky eye.

Smoky eye shadow can enhance any look, day or night. Also, remember that a smoky eye is not limited to black or ultra dark shadow colors either. A smoky eye can be done with any color of shadows using the same application and technique.

Here is a brief explanation of how to get that sexy, sultry, smoky eye:

- First, prep the eyelids with primer so the makeup will hold. Doing this keeps eye shadow from melting into your eyelid creases. Wait until the primer is settled before applying any eye makeup.
- Apply eyeliner above the upper eyelash line, drawing the line thicker in the middle of the eye to the outer corner.
- Blend in the color on the bottom, which is the key to the smoky eye look. Use a kohl eyeliner pencil. This is easier to smudge. Use a Q-tip to smudge it or a bit of shadow for a full smudged look. Great traditional colors are black, dark brown, and grey.

- Use a light color on the base of the eye. The trick is to pair a lighter base with the darker color. Put the light color on the eyelids, onwards to the brow bone. I like taupe and pearl as a base color.
- Blend in the darker color. Keep dark color below the crease line with the base color and eyeliner on; you can begin to create the smoky eye effect. Use a darker shadow in the corners to the crease of eye. Use an eye shadow brush and blend color, starting at your eyelash line, blending upwards. Make sure it's blended well so the eyeliner disappears. The key is blending and avoiding harsh lines.
- Apply several coats of mascara, and you're done. For a more dramatic effect, false eyelashes can be applied. With practice, this look can be done in 15 minutes or less.

Below: Smoky Eye Technique

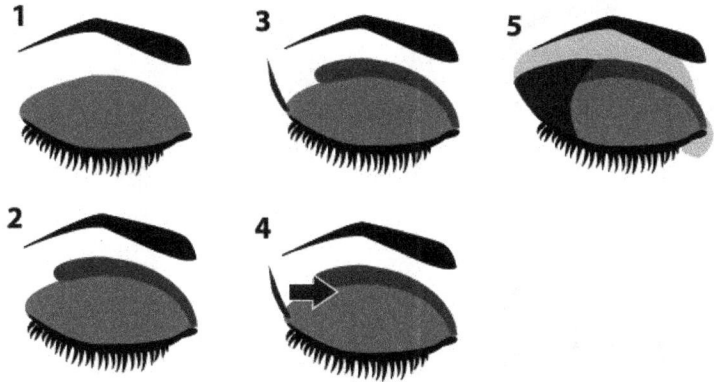

CAT EYE TECHNIQUE

The cat eye technique can be achieved by using usually a

black liner, pigment, pencil, or shadow. There are many variations of the cat eye, depending on the look you are trying to achieve. (You can add your own personal touch to create the desired look.) Here is a basic technique:

- Line the upper eyelash line with black liner or desired color from the inner corners to the outer corners of your eyes.
- Extend the line beyond the eye, but no further than the tip of your eyebrows. Also, the lower eyelash line can be lined and extended to the outer corners of the eye.
- For a dramatic effect, the liner can be extended outwards to blend in with the line on upper eyelash line. Always practice.
- The key is to try to get a perfectly smooth line.

Below: Cat Eye Technique (European R-L)

PUPPY EYE TECHNIQUE

The puppy eye is the exact opposite of the cat eye look and technique. The look will make your eyes appear demure and sweet, while creating the appearance of rounder and larger eyes. Instead of the eyeliner being drawn upwards, the eyeliner extends downwards, following the natural slope of the shape of the eye. And instead of the vampy and seductive effect of the cat eye look, the puppy eye is all about innocence. Many people find this technique less difficult to achieve on their own than the cat eye. In terms of the looks themselves, I personally love them both.

Below is the technique for the puppy eye look:

- Using a black pencil eyeliner or liquid, line the upper eyelash line from the inner corners to about mid-eye.
- Once you get to the end of the eye, gradually extend the line in a downward direction.
- Line your outer lower eyelash line, extending the liner to meet the upper lash liner to form a triangle shape.
- Fill in the small triangle, and then layer the area with black liquid liner or whatever color is being used.
- For longevity, apply black shadow over it, especially for a long night out! Tap the shadow in with a small eye shadow brush for a heavier application. Remember less is more so start out with a small amount and apply until you achieve your desired look! Use black pencil eyeliner on the inside of the eyes at the bottom or lower lids.

11

Below: Puppy Eye Technique

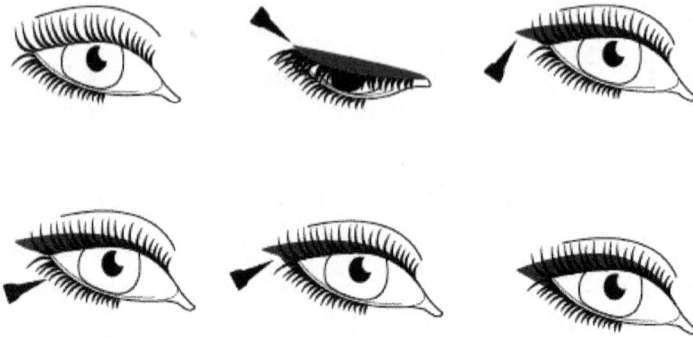

DEFINITIONS OF EYE ENHANCING COLORS

Highlighter is the lightest shade used in all eye looks. This enhances the features of the eyes, such as the brow bone and the inner corners of the eyes. Highlighter adds a burst of color and makes the eye appear more open for a "wide-eyed" effect.

Mid-tones are the medium shades used in all eye looks. These shades are usually neutral colors such as taupe, tan, or beige. These colors are great alone for daytime looks. Just add mascara.

Accent colors are usually the darkest shade used in all eye looks. By adding accent colors, a pop of color and depth is added to the eyes.

EYELASH APPLICATIONS

If you are blessed with naturally long, thick eyelashes, all that is needed is several coats of mascara and an eyelash curler. Depending on the look of the season, mascara can be smooth and exact, or clumpy and heavy. Both looks are trending at different times during the seasons; however, traditional, clean mascara always looks best.

False eyelashes can be applied using safe adhesive, made for eyelash strips and individual eyelash extension application. Trim the corners of the eyelash strip extension by cutting off the very edge of the eyelash strip. Then, apply a small amount of eyelash glue. More glue can be applied if needed. Try to avoid the glue becoming tacky because it will clump. Place the eyelash strip very close to the base of your eyelashes. Make sure the eyelash strip is from the corner of the natural eyelash line and extends to the end of the natural eyelash line. Anything outside of the natural eyelash line will look artificial. Allow the glue to dry for at least a minute before applying mascara to fuse both your natural eyelashes and the false eyelashes together.

Individual eyelash extensions can be applied as well, using tweezers, glue, a steady hand, and a great deal of practice! If you are not a professional or are unfamiliar with this technique, consult a professional cosmetologist, esthetician, or eyelash expert to have this application done.

FALSE EYELASHES HAIRS

Human Hairs: Looks and feels natural.

Synthetic Hairs: Usually course.

Mink hairs: Soft, shiny, and full. Feels lighter when worn. In most cases, it can be used repeatedly with proper care for the eyelashes.

Siberian Sable Hairs: Fluffy and full. Feels much lighter when worn. In most cases, it can be used repeatedly with proper care for the eyelashes.

Silk: Sleek and shiny.

3D Eyelashes: Exaggerated, very defined. Are usually made with most hair types.

TIPS & TRICKS

- Always blend eye shadows. The colors should blend smoothly together. Avoid streaks of color and harsh lines.
- If uncertain of your eye shape, just use the application for almond shape eyes, which are considered "standard." This technique works well for all eyes.
- For individuals with combination eye types, simply choose the eye shapes that apply best and use the applications for the features you want to enhance or minimize.

RECOMENDED TOOLS

- Medium, rounded eyebrow blending brush
- Small eyebrow brush for defining eyebrows
- Small, angled, fluffy eye shadow brush for blending
- Small contouring brush
- Small, soft, eye shadow brush with flat tip
- Small eye shadow brush with soft, round tip
- Concealer brush
- Eyebrow brush

- Mascara wand
- Cotton swabs for clean ups
- Eyelash curler
- Eyebrow gel

CHAPTER 2: U MAKE ME BLUSH

The art to giving good face is enhancing your best features. Blushing is a natural reaction that is caused when we are excited, embarrassed, or happy. Blush can also look natural when applied correctly.

There are several different ways to apply blush to your cheeks. The concept is to create the look of rosiness without it being overdone. In some cases, such as film and television, blush should be applied heavier so that it reads well on camera.

Blush should be applied underneath your cheekbones, extending no further than the corner of the eye. The product should be applied with soft upward strokes. Avoid harsh lines. The color needs to blend and harmonize well into your natural complexion while exposing a hint of color to brighten your face. Highlighter can be applied on top of your cheekbones for an illuminating effect. Choose colors that complement your complexion. Peach blush colors are ideal for every complexion.

For a fresh-faced look, blush can be applied to the apples of your cheeks. The apples of your cheeks are the parts of the cheeks that stand out when you smile. A light sweep of color should be applied to just the apples of the cheek. This look is great for daytime makeup, or if you just want to look refreshed without appearing to be overdone.

Blush should always be pretty and natural looking. Be careful—if overdone or applied incorrectly, blush can have a clown-like appearance. Rose water and other blush stains can be used as well. I personally like cheek stains for a subtle, natural flush to the face.

Powder blush can have staying power if primer is used, but can come off easily due to perspiration. Primer is a lightweight formula used before makeup is applied to the face. Primer acts as a bond between the makeup and the skin. Cream blush works well because of the consistency and the texture. Be careful with cream blush because it can go on extremely heavy, so be sure to use a small amount first and apply more if needed to achieve your desired look. Remember to always blend so it enhances and accentuates the cheekbones.

TIPS & TRICKS

- By combining powder blush and petroleum jelly, you can create cream blush.
- Lipstick can also be used as a cream blush as well by dabbing on color lightly with your finger. Maximize on your products for other functions.
- Fingers can be used for application of cream blush. Please make sure to always have clean hands before applying.

RECOMMENDED TOOLS

- Large fluffy powder brush
- Large fluffy blush brush
- Medium blush brush
- Medium powder brush

CHAPTER 3: GIVING FACE

There aren't many rules when it comes to contouring and highlighting. The trick to perfect contouring begins with learning your face. When you learn your face, you discover what features you would like to minimize and which features you want to maximize.

The concentration areas include cheekbones, bow of the lips, and eyes for highlighting, and the nose, forehead, and chin for contouring. Determine the shape of your face, whether it is round, oval, square, pear, or heart. By identifying this and understanding your facial structure, it will be easier to manipulate and accentuate your features.

First, choose a contouring kit. This is something available at beauty retail stores. Because of the color palette, it will much easier to understand which colors go where. Included in the palette should be contouring and highlighting creams in colors that harmonize well with your complexion.

Next, choose a highlighting set of colors. The highlighting set will consist of colors that will illuminate your face. These colors are included in the contouring palette. Usually, I use a gold or iridescent shimmer afterwards to make some area stand out in different lighting, or when I know that I am going to be photographed.

BEAUTY SIDEBAR: STROBING

Highlighting can be done alone without using darker colors or contouring. This technique is known as "Strobing." Strobing involves highlighting your face without the dramatic look of heavy contouring. The strobing technique is used to illuminate the skin by layering on highlights of product to achieve a glowing complexion—not be confused with bronzing or contouring. Highlighter is applied to areas of your face to create a radiant glow.

My suggestion is to figure out where the light best highlights your face and apply the product to those areas. These areas usually include cheekbones extending to the temple area, down the center of your nose, chin, and bow of lips, as well as any area that you want highlighted. For fair skin, use white, pink, and beige tones. For medium skin, use bronze and gold tones. And for darker skin tones, use peach, gold, and orange tones for highlighting. Instantly, your face will light up!

Below: Strobing Technique

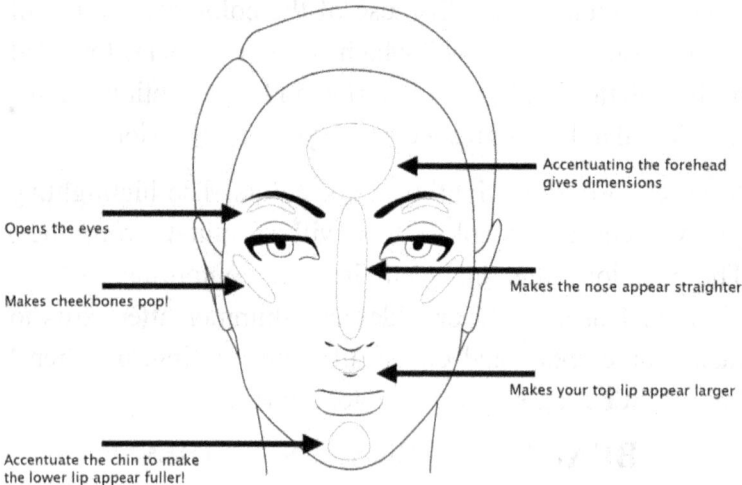

Accentuating the forehead gives dimensions

Opens the eyes

Makes cheekbones pop!

Makes the nose appear straighter

Makes your top lip appear larger

Accentuate the chin to make the lower lip appear fuller!

Choose a bronzer or highlighter that will flatter your face. For contouring, choose a darker shade, and for highlighting, use lighter shades. Dark powder, cream, or foundations work well for dramatic contouring and highlighting. These colors will be available in the contouring sets.

For contouring your cheekbones, draw a soft line underneath your cheekbones and blend downwards along the line of your cheekbone.

For contouring your nose, draw a line down both sides of your nose and blend outward until the line is faint but still visible. Chose a lighter color from the contouring kit and draw a line down the center of your nose starting at the top of the nose and blend. Avoid heavy lines. It's not cute! Blending is the key.

For foreheads, choose a darker powder, cream, or foundation from your contouring kit. After you have chosen your color, draw triangle shapes on the side of the forehead. For square, pear, and round faces, contour larger, deeper triangle shapes to create an oval shape effect for your face.

Use concealer for added touch-ups after the contouring technique is finished. You may want to add more concealer underneath your eyes, or anywhere that you feel needs more coverage. Also, if you feel that some areas need more contouring, repeat the steps above until your desired look is achieved. The same rules apply for highlighting as well.

Blend well. Apply your usual makeup routine once everything is blended to perfection. Once again, practice makes perfect! Live tutorials are always available online if you need a visual demonstration.

Below: Face Shapes for Contouring Technique

  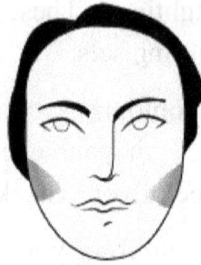

Heart   Oblong   Oval

  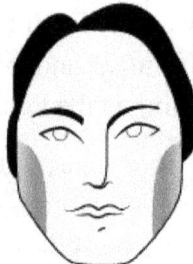

Round   Square   Diamond

THINGS THAT ARE TACKY

- Two-toned face and neck (makeup should be blended well so it doesn't look like you're wearing a mask)
- Harsh lines
- Dirty makeup sponges or brushes (they harbor bacteria and can cause major breakouts)

RECOMMENDED TOOLS

- Application sponges
- Beauty blenders
- Large foundation brush
- Concealer brush

CHAPTER 4: PUCKER UP

For a kissable mouth, lips should always appear inviting. The shape of your lips can be manipulated to look fuller or smaller by using some simple makeup techniques.

For the appearance of larger lips, lip liner should be applied at the base of the natural lip line using a nude pencil to create the outline. Once the shape of the lip is defined using the nude lip liner, I then use the desired color of lip liner over the nude lip liner until the nude color disappears. After this is done, lipstick can now be applied. Make sure the color stays within the boundaries of your lips. Gloss can then be applied in a similar hue to create the illusion of fuller lips.

For the appearance of smaller lips, foundation can be applied on the lips using a sponge or makeup brush. Once this is done, your lip liner should be applied directly under the natural lip line. Matte lipstick is best for this look. Lip-gloss will only give the illusion a larger appearance.

For a pouty mouth, lip-gloss should be applied to the center of the mouth on both the top and bottom of your lips to create the pouty look.

Exfoliating the lips is very important. By exfoliating, dead, dry, and chapped skin is removed from your lips. The results are smooth, supple lips. Lip-gloss, lip liners, and lipsticks will go on smoother and the appearance will be gorgeous! To exfoliate your lips, use a toothbrush, and gently brush your lips in a back and forth motion. Sugar or baking soda can be used for exfoliation. Rinse and moisturize your lips generously with lip balm. This will help reduce the appearance of lines, and also cracked and dry lips. The result is rosy, soft, and residue-free lips that not only look amazing with or without lipstick, but also very kissable!

THINGS THAT ARE TACKY

- Residue on your lips
- Cakey lipstick or gloss
- Lip liner drawn on far outside the natural lip line
- Old tubes of lip-gloss and lipstick (lip-gloss wands tend to develop an odor over time)
- Dirty product caps and tubes
- Sharing any lip products other than lip pencils (the point can be broken and can then be sharpened for a new point)
- Dry mouth
- Bad breath
- Stained or yellow teeth
- Overly greasy or glossy lips (only slather on the lip moisturizer during bedtime, at the beach, or in cold weather)

CHAPTER 5: WHEN THE CLOCK STRIKES 12

Transition makeup is essential for transforming your day makeup look into an evening look for a soirée or event. If you are unable to go to a makeup artist and have your face transformed, then these tips will be helpful in a scenario like this.

Most of the time, daytime makeup isn't heavy or full-faced. Usually, it's just the basics, which are: foundation, mascara, lip color, sometimes blush, and subtle eyebrow fill-ins (depending on the eyebrows).

Most women who are transitioning from day to evening makeup are usually at work. So, makeup most of the time is and should be minimum, depending on your profession and how much makeup you feel comfortable wearing on your face.

So, now that you're headed out for a night on the town, your makeup must reflect an evening feel. The most common thing to do is to make sure your foundation is still intact and refresh it. A compact with loose or pressed power is sufficient for touch-ups. The use of eye shadows and eyeliner can be applied to dramatize the eyes. Lip color should be changed to a shade of red, burgundy, or a deep, bold color that is suitable for the look your are trying to achieve. Also, make sure the color complements your skin tone. Blush should also be a tad bit heavier, and highlighters can be used to accentuate features such as your cheekbones.

Whatever color palette you decide to use, the key is making sure the makeup is bolder and always beautiful. Personally, I prefer dark eyes with a visible, lighter-colored lipstick and red, or darker-colored lips without heavy blush application. I always use mascara during the day or evening. Mascara can transition from day to night instantly. It is the one universal product that can be used for both occasions.

CHAPTER 6: FLAWLESS

Achieving a flawless face takes time and practice. The more you do it, the easier it becomes. Flawless is everything. Flawless is perfection. Flawless knows that your face will be unforgettable in pictures, in person, and in the mirror when you look at yourself. The focus on achieving a flawless face begins with clean, moisturized skin.

After your skin has absorbed the moisturizer, primer should then be applied evenly to your face. Once that settles, concealer should be applied only to areas that need the extra coverage. I like to use a tiny concealer makeup brush that can be used for harder areas, like under my eyes. Using a foundation brush, sponge, beauty blender or your hands and fingers, the foundation should be placed all over your face evenly, including the jawline, and then lightly feathering down onto your neck, with very light strokes until it is transparent.

Foundation should never sit on top of your face. It creates a "muddy" look, and that should make sense to most women who understand and have seen this before on others. Foundation has to blend as close as possible to your natural skin tone, even if you have a tan.

Additionally, once this step is completed, you can use concealer again to go over missed spots or areas that you feel may need more coverage, even after the foundation is applied. Remember to tap the concealer onto the desired areas and blend well so the product disappears. It doesn't matter if you see the color difference in the concealer because it is supposed to be a shade lighter than your skin tone and foundation. This will brighten the darker areas, such as under eye circles and blemishes.

The makeup application will vary, depending on what look you are trying to achieve. The basic rule of being flawless is that even if you did not add any additional makeup to your face, your foundation should be perfect.

CHAPTER 7: SUNKISSED

Tanning—friend or foe? I say…friend! Although I am guilty of being a sun worshiper, I do not recommend exposing your skin to the harsh UV rays of the sun often. Vitamin D is great, and is also a natural vitamin that the sun provides. However, too much sun is damaging and causes an array of problems such as wrinkling, sunburn, and even cancer.

Traditionally, the sun has been the source of achieving the perfect tan. Laying on the beach or poolside has been a favorite pastime for most of us. Unfortunately, the sunrays are and can be damaging to the skin. Wrinkling, sunspots, premature aging, and leathery skin are all effects of the sunrays. Fortunately, there is a happy alternative to achieve this desired look.

Here are some steps to use bronzers and self-tanners that will help give off that sun-kissed look and keep your skin healthy and glowing:

- First, shave or wax and exfoliate your entire body. This will ensure that the product used will be applied evenly and the skin is smooth.

- Second, apply bronzer or self-tanner to the skin, starting at the feet and apply upward. Also, spray tanning (airbrushing) works well for an even tan. For best results, I would suggest to be sprayed in the nude, unless you want tan lines.

- Third, after your application is completely dry, you can then use a bronzer or dusting power to add shimmer and illuminate specific areas to your body. This will enhance some areas that you may want to stand out, such as the décolletage area (the space above and in between the breast area) .

This procedure should last for up to a week if properly maintained. Also, moisturizing is essential once the application is completely dry. Spray tans are great for all completions. The color has to be two shades darker than your natural complexion with hues of gold to create the sun-kissed effect. Self-tanning also camouflages stretch marks and blemished areas, and leaves your complexion even and beautiful without the harsh effects of too much sun.

A good tan while on vacation is always perfect for sun-kissed skin as well. Stay hydrated with plenty of water and use sunblock with high levels of SPF if you're going to tan in the sun.

THINGS THAT ARE TACKY

- Missed spots that reveal your true complexion

- Orange-colored skin

- Un-tanned feet while the rest of your body is a different color.

- A completely pale ass and tanned body (unless you're wearing a bikini and going for that look of having tan lines)

- Burnt, leathery, sun-damaged skin

CHAPTER 8: BEDTIME RITUALS

I hate to sound redundant and like a screaming parent, but you must wash your face before bedtime! Makeup can clog your pores and irritate your skin. There are some exceptions to the rule. For example, if you are extremely inebriated and not functional, then yes, you can have a hall pass and wash your face in the morning. Another example would be if you are being engaged in seduction and happen to fall asleep afterwards (it must be really good), then yes, you can have a hall pass for this as well. Otherwise, wash your face!

Facial wash and makeup remover wipes are best for removing makeup. Products such as baby oil or petroleum jelly can be used to remove eye makeup effectively. It also works well for removing mascara and hard-to-remove lipstick and lip stains.

For dry skin, any products with heavy amounts of alcohol should be avoided. Mild gentle facial wash is recommended. For oily skin, any products that absorb oil should be used to control overactive sebaceous glands that cause breakouts. For normal skin, most products are sufficient for removing makeup.

Avoid harsh soaps that could potentially disrupt the skin. Some skin types are more sensitive than others. I am not suggesting that regular soap cannot be used if that is all that is available, but if there are choices, opt instead for facial cleanser or makeup removal wipes.

After makeup removal, depending on your skin type, toner is a great product to use. Toner closes the pores and leaves your skin feeling refreshed. After this step, you should moisturize with a cream or lotion that is rich in vitamin E and C. Once again, depending on the type of skin you have, the cream or lotion should be a formula that is perfect for your skin type. Heavier creams and lotions should be used for dry skin types, and lighter creams and lotions should be used for oily skin. Make sure to apply the moisturizer in an upward motion. This technique helps to keep the skin from sagging downwards and also helps to maintain muscle tone in your face. Always moisturize the neck area as well.

It is important to use moisturizer around the eye area. This should be applied counter-clockwise and will reduce the appearance of fine lines and wrinkles.

If needed, acne creams and pimple solutions should be applied afterwards. My own personal technique is to take a Q-tip and use a dab of witch hazel or peroxide to the infected area and the apply the acne cream.

This beauty ritual will ensure clean, fresh, healthy skin in the morning.

CHAPTER 9: FIRST DATE

We all experience many firsts in our lives that are memorable. These experiences, such as graduations, proms, special events, dates, etc., will forever be embedded in our lives because of pictures, memorabilia, and just plain memory! This is why you should always want to look and feel your best.

First date makeup should be pretty and never overdone. Because makeup can totally transform your look, remember that it eventually has to come off and you would always want to look like yourself with the makeup on. Accenting your best features, which include cheekbones, eyes, and lips are key pointers to remember.

Overdone and ultra dramatic makeup can sometimes make your face look animated and like a circus freak! Also, at the end of the night, it can rub off on your date's clothes—that is not a good thing.

Highlighting your cheekbones with illuminators and using BB and CC creams will make your cheekbones pop. Contouring is also a plus to create a sultry, sexy look, which is great for evening affairs. Full-face foundation application will even out your skin tone. Use concealer to cover up the usual suspects, which include dark circles, blemishes, and pimples.

Lips should always look inviting. The use of matte lip colors is wonderful because the lipstick has staying power. Remember to use a lip balm to keep your lips hydrated underneath. Matte lipsticks, depending on the formula, have a tendency to dry the lips. Make sure that the lip balm is thoroughly saturated into the lips before applying matte colors and lip liners. Lips should never be greasy before applying a matte lip color. It is helpful when you're eating, drinking, and kissing.

The use of cheek color and blush is always essential. The application of blush should be slightly below the cheekbone with the highlighter on top of the cheekbone. Eye shadows, eyeliners, and false eyelashes and extensions can be worn also.

Foundation should be flawless and even, and there should never be any lines of demarcation (meaning when your neck and face do not match). A full face of makeup can be worn during a date in the evening. Remember to always excuse yourself and use the ladies' room for makeup touch-ups.

For special events, evening engagements, and proms, always go with a heavier application, but remember to make sure that all the makeup is well blended and the colors harmonize.

Lip-glosses are fresh and natural looking for dates during the daytime. Eyeliners can be worn also. Eye shadow color is usually not necessary for daytime dating, unless it is an extremely light color that looks very natural.

Blush application is optional, but if you must, apply it to the apples of your cheeks and blend it well so it appears natural. Cheek and lip stains are also a great product to use as well for a natural flushed finish.

Foundation or tinted moisturizer can be used to even out the skin tone. Use concealer for under-eye circles and to cover pimples, blemishes, and other things you may want hidden and camouflaged. These tips also apply to graduation ceremonies and just about any daytime event.

THINGS THAT ARE TACKY

- Lipstick color on the teeth
- False eyelashes that have been used over and over again and have excessive amounts of old mascara and adhesive on them
- The foundation line that stops at your jawline and is a totally different color from your neck
- Makeup application at the dinner table
- Picking your teeth with your nails in public
- Raccoon eyes
- Lipstick above the natural lip line
- Chipped nail polish

CHAPTER 10: MEET THE PARENTS

When it is time to be introduced to parents, family members, or any person that may require a formal or semi-formal introduction, the first impression is a lasting one in most cases. Makeup should always reflect the occasion, whether it is a holiday or family dinner, job interview, or any event that you may be judged the first time upon entering one of these types of situations.

Meeting the parents can put a great deal of pressure on anyone, so it is important to look and act your best. Makeup should be minimal and not overdone. Makeup can be worn as a tool to enhance your best features and camouflage any imperfections. Tinted moisturizer is a great product to use, combined with concealer just to cover imperfections such as a pimple, discoloration, or a scar. Foundations should be lightweight and not cakey or overly heavy as if you were wearing a mask. After all, cakey makeup shows every wrinkle, and the solution settles into your skin. This can cause your face to look much older and, in some cases, dry. Heavy foundations can make you look oily, overdone, and cartoonish.

Looking flawless can be achieved with a full makeup application, but it doesn't look have to look like you are going out to a club or a Halloween party. If you are wearing eye shadows or liners, the colors should be soft and subtle. Beige and taupe colors are a great combination if you must wear a smoky eye. Eyeliner can be worn, but avoid the over exaggerated winged cat-eye. It may not be the time or place or an appropriate look for the occasion. Instead, wear eyeliner on the top or bottom of your lids, or both. The liner should not extend far beyond the outer corners of your eyes. Try to use black, brown, or grey liners. Avoid bright colors—they may look tacky and inappropriate.

White or gold shimmer and eye shadow can be used to make the eyes appear more open, but use it sparingly. Two light coats of black or brown mascara will be just enough for your lashes. Leave the exaggerated falsies at home, but if you must wear false eyelashes, opt for a natural looking pair or try eyelash extensions.

Eyebrows are important. Eyebrows frame your face and can transform your makeup application entirely. It is important to remember to fill in eyebrows if your hairs are thin or non-existent. Thicker eyebrows can be worn natural with slight fill-ins to look precise.

Cheeks should be bare or slightly rosy. Soft pinks, berry, and peach are the color palettes that would be most appropriate. Blush application should be done with a light stroke. A sweep of color to brighten the face is all that is needed. Some highlighting and contouring can be done, depending on the occasion, but should still be minimal and not overly defining.

For minimizing foreheads and noses, apply the makeup as you would normally for contouring, (See Chapter 3) but avoid harsh lines. Make sure the makeup is well blended. Remember to always enhance and bring out your best features.

For lips, a variety of colors can be used. Stay away from overly bright and neon colors. Red lips can sometimes be taboo for certain occasions.

Interviews can be tricky. Depending on what field you are

in and position you may be interviewing for, red lips may be a bit too much. Some safe colors include nude, light pink, brick reds, and light- to medium-plum colors. Lipglosses can be used over lipstick or worn alone. Lip liners should not have heavy lines outside the natural lip line or a harsh, thick distinct line, unless you are using the ombré technique (which I explain later in Chapter 11). I would not recommend this look for meeting the parents.

THINGS THAT ARE TACKY

- Overexposed cleavage in front of his dad, or at a corporate or formal function
- Overly done makeup
- Overpowering perfume

CHAPTER 11: SEDUCE HIM

Seduction can be interpreted in many ways. There is certainly an art to it! The bedroom, the living room, bathroom, and yes, even the kitchen can be as seductive as you want it to be.

Seduction is setting the mood and tone of an intimate atmosphere. Burning candles, dim lights, a bottle of your favorite wine or champagne, or drink of choice, soft music, and rose petals are just the ambiance. But what about you? Your makeup should be a reflection of however you are feeling.

Now, I am not suggesting that you go to bed with a full face of makeup, but you can certainly slide into the sheets looking fabulous! Makeup should always be pretty and beautiful, especially for seduction. The eyes should look exotic and brows should be arched to perfection. Lips should be suggestive and flirty, yet look good enough to eat. Perfect hygiene is a must, and skin should always be smooth and soft, legs, underarm, and pubic hair should be manicured like a lush lawn, unless your partner likes it otherwise.

Red and pink lip color, whether it's lipstick or lip-gloss is always a sexy color. Ruby reds and pops of pinks are great colors for seduction. Eyes can be nude with a few coats of mascara on the lashes to create a seducing eye. But, a smoky eye is always a winner! Remember, eyes are the window to the soul. Sexy eyes are one of the most seductive features on a person's face, so be sure to play them up.

Experiment with color, but nothing too bright or circus-esque. I have explained two distinctly different looks for seduction. Depending on what look you're going for, here are two surefire makeup applications that will guarantee seduction:

The art to seduction begins with sexy lips and sultry eyes. This can be achieved by two different approaches to makeup, which are the **Vixen** and the **Virgin**. Depending on what role you are playing, these makeup techniques will help set the mood in your quest for seduction.

For the **Vixen**, makeup should be vampy and lips should be prominent. The use of reds, burgundy, vibrant pinks, and nudes should match your inner seductress. This is a great time to use all of your products without looking overdone. Foundation, creams, concealers, bronzers, and highlighters can all be used in ways to create a perfect picture of seduction. Your face should be "beat." This means your face should be flawless. There should be any blemishes, visible under-eye circles, or pimples, etc., anywhere in sight.

Eyelashes should be exaggerated and hypnotizing, either with several coats of mascara or using eyelash strips or eyelash extensions. I recommend 3D false lashes and Mink or Siberian Sable false eyelashes for this look. Cheekbones and temples should be highlighted with bronzer or iridescent powder to bring out your features. Eyebrows should be filled in and arched to perfection using eye shadows or eyebrow wax.

The technique used for sultry lips is known as the ombré effect. Similar to the popular hair color technique, ombré combines two or three similar colors and combine them until they are blended well and harmonized. Experiment with different makeup applications and techniques! The center of the lips for the ombré effect can be a different shade outside of your original colors you chose for this look. Lips can also be painted in one of the classic reds: brick reds, deep reds, tomato red, and yes, blood red. Midnight blue, navy. burgundy and darker shades are also a great alternative for trying something daring and bold.

The smoky eye shadow technique or a winged cat eye on the top lid should also be incorporated. Eyes are extremely important for Vixen makeup. Highlighter or white shimmer powder in the inner corners of your eyes and feathered out slightly onto the top and bottom corners also. For deeper skin tones, a great alternative is bronze shimmer powder. Remember, makeup should be fun and creative but always pretty and well blended.

For the **Virgin**, makeup should be soft and angelic. Hues of pale pinks and nudes are the color palette of choice. The face should be clean and even toned without the use of heavy makeup for highlighting. Cheekbones can be highlighted and defined – however, the colors should be blended to perfection so it appears as if your glow is as natural as possible. Tinted moisturizer, foundations, and creams can be used as a base for the face. The skin should be glowing, radiant, and natural before the makeup application. Subtle highlighting and light shimmering touches are essential for this look.

Lips can be stained with rose water topped with a soft nude or pink lip color, preferably lip-gloss. Pouty lips are a "must have." This is done by applying a lighter shade of lip color in the center of your lips. Eye shadows in shades of milk chocolate, taupe, vanilla, and beige should be swept across the eyelid only. White eyeliner can also be used to make the eyes appear larger. By highlighting the brow bone underneath using a pale shimmer shadow, this gives the arch a wow factor and makes your eyebrows appear more defined. An eye pencil or eyebrow wax can be used for fill-ins between brow hairs. Eye shadow can sometimes look too heavy when applied for brows, unless you have had plenty of practice.

Eyelash extensions or natural eyelashes are best for the Virgin. Apply a few coats of mascara to your natural eyelashes for length and volume. Eyelash extensions need to look natural and "doe-like." The apples of the cheeks can be lightly dusted with a hint of peach, light pinks, or similar colors, depending on your complexion. Apply a shimmery powder or bronzer to the décollaté area. Your makeup should look effortless and beautiful.

MAKEUP TIPS

Highlighting the center of the décollaté (which is the top of the chest, extending down above the center of the cleavage area) is always sexy and can be incorporated in any makeup look that exposes some skin. This requires the use of décollaté shimmer powder or liquid, which are available in iridescent shades and bronze shades for an ultra feminine pop!

THINGS THAT ARE TACKY

- Dingy or dirty sheets and bed linens
- Unpleasant smells or overpowering perfumes and sprays

- Animal hair everywhere
- Unflattering, drawn on, pencil thin eyebrows
- Wigs, hair pieces, false eyelashes, colored contact lenses, and other add-ons lying around on a nightstand after the moment ends
- Stained undergarments
- Bad breath
- Excessive vomiting and rowdy, drunk behavior
- Passing gas, a.k.a. farting. Hold it in until you excuse yourself, unless you're married, common law husband and wife, life partner or ultra comfortable around one another that you both do not mind smelling egg salad, harsh chemicals, or garbage.
- Be sure to cleanse thoroughly after bowl movements. Your partner may want to explore.

CHAPTER 12: "WAKE UP" MAKEUP

The art to "wake up makeup" is simple, and so is the makeup technique to achieve this rosy, dewy flushed look as if your cheeks were pinched and your lips were just bitten. These rules apply if you are waking up next to a potential beau, a one-night stand (if you care that much), or have visitors who will see you in the morning or running errands or just because!

A clean, healthy glow is the best wake up look to have. So, always remember to wash your face and moisturize after makeup removal and treat problem areas. Smart skin is healthy skin!

But, like the saying goes, "Fake it till you make it." Wake up makeup gives the illusion as if you not wearing any makeup at all.

The application of makeup (foundation, concealer, and BB creams) should be limited and applied only to the area that needs to be covered. For example, if you have a pimple, dab a dot of concealer on the area and blend until the edges melt into your skin. The rest of your face should be clean, clear, and moisturized.

For rosy cheeks and lips, I like to use a rose water stain on my cheeks and lips, followed by a dab of lip balm and Vaseline. The combination makes your skin appear to be flushed, glowing, and rosy. There are plenty of rose water and gel stains on the market to accommodate your look.

Mascara can be used in moderation. A light single coat does the trick. This will always make your eyes pop and look sultry, even early in the morning.

Eyebrows should always be groomed and neat. This can be achieved by using an eyebrow gel to tame unruly brow hairs. Or, you can do a light fill in. For sparse browns, use brow wax. It looks natural and doesn't rub off easily.

Once this is finished, you can slide back into bed and wake up even more beautiful than you already are. He will never know; they will never know. It's a technique that is a best-kept secret! #wakeupmakeup

THINGS THAT ARE TACKY

- Unshaved underarms
- Hairy legs
- Ultra dry skin (old fashion petroleum jelly works every time)
- Stubble
- Overly greasy hair and body (moisturizing is the key to youthful and radiant skin, so don't skimp but use just enough—the sheets shouldn't be soaked or soiled)
- Uni-brows
- Sparse eyebrows
- Used and last night's eyelash falsies with dried glue still on them
- Feminine products, including tampons and sanitary napkins, visible anywhere!
- Eye boogers
- Not so fresh morning breath (after all, if you're going to apply a little makeup, you can at least brush your teeth or use mouthwash)

CHAPTER 13: HERE COMES THE BRIDE

Today is your special day, or it's someone else's special day and you are a major part of it! Bridal makeup can vary, depending on the bride, the wedding theme, and personal style. Most brides go through a series of makeup tutorials before choosing their makeup.

I know about this firsthand. One of my best friends was adamant about her makeup for her wedding. As a makeup artist, bridesmaid, and best friend, I was at her beck and call. We live about an hour away from each other, and I made several trips to her house to test and try out makeup colors for her wedding day. After about three or four trips to see her, we finally figured out what colors she wanted to use and what look she was going for.

I always tell my clients who are brides to go with what feels most natural. There isn't anything wrong with experimenting with color; however, you do not want a makeup disaster the day of the wedding. It is important to try different looks to figure out what will be right for you. Remember, the wedding pictures are permanent and cannot be changed, so choose your makeup palette wisely.

Bridal makeup should be gorgeous, beautiful, and pretty. Foundation should be flawless. Contouring and highlighting is a must. Makeup should never be too heavy, especially if you're having an outdoor wedding in the summer months when it is hot outside. Makeup will completely melt off your face and perhaps onto your dress, the groom, or a guest.

A full face of makeup is required to look your best in photos. Apply the whole kit and caboodle. Primer should be used to hold the makeup together. False eyelashes can be worn to accentuate the eyes if you feel comfortable wearing them. The use of eye shadow and eyeliner play a key role in your makeup application. Decide if you want a smoky eye or a hint of color to play up your eyes. Cheekbones should be contoured, highlighted, and rosy. Powder and blot paper is great for shine. Too much powder can leave your skin looking dull and cakey, so remember to dust and apply more if needed.

A strong lip color looks great with a nude or neutral color face. A pale or nude lip looks great with anything. When taking pictures, it is important to have your makeup read well in the photos. If you choose to have a makeup artist, make sure you invite them to the wedding for touch-ups!

Whatever you decide on your special day, make sure you look and feel flawless. That's what's most important!

Also, as a bridesmaid, your makeup should never clash with your dress and should always be tasteful. After all, you are in the photos, which last a lifetime.

THINGS THAT ARE TACKY

- Old, clumpy eyelash extensions (remove them or have them done over)
- Used eyelash strips. I know they are your best pair, the glue isn't coming off, and you have had them on for a few days, but invest in a new pair. I recommend #prettygirlgangcosmetics Mink or Siberian Sable eyelash strips and Mink individual eyelashes for lash-extension applications. The eyelashes are re-usable up to twenty times, 100%

hypoallergenic, animal cruelty free, and affordable.

- Neon-colored makeup anywhere
- Remove face piercings, if possible (they can be a distraction)
- Dingy lingerie
- Too long, claw-like nails
- Runs in stockings (keep an extra pair with a bridesmaid or your mother)
- Gaudy unattractive cheap costume jewelry

CHAPTER 14: AROUND THE WORLD & BACK

During my visits to different parts of the world, I have made a conscious effort to experience the spas of the hotels that I have stayed in. Each city, country, or continent has its own traditions, minerals, herbs, and blends that makeup the rituals and ingredients used for spa treatments. In this chapter, I will share my unique experiences in various spas around the world.

FISH SPA PEDICURES: WATERTOWN, SHANGHAI, CHINA

Fish Spa pedicures, or the fish doctor, is the latest new trend in pedicure treatments. The fad has hit the U.S and is now popular in many salons across the country. Recently, I visited Watertown in Shanghai, China and I got to see what it was actually like up close and personal. Although I did not participate in the trendy ritual, it looked interesting, and I asked plenty of questions about the procedure.

The fish spa pedicure treatment originated in Turkey. It quickly spread to China where it became available at most salons. Currently, there are a few salons across the U.S. offering this treatment. The procedure starts with a pedicure bowl filled with warm water. The water contains small fish called Garra Rufa, often referred to as "doctor fish." The fish then eat away at the dead skin on the feet, producing soft and smooth feet. Unlike the traditional pedicure that lasts for two to three weeks, the fish pedicure has longer sustainability.

The price range varies between $45 to $95 per treatment. It

usually lasts about 20 to 30 minutes, depending on which salon you visit. Treatment is suggested every three months to help skin conditions such as eczema, psoriasis, and dermatitis.

Owners of these fish spas have stated that pedicure treatment is completely sanitary. The water is changed after each patron, and the same fish are sometimes put back into the basin with fresh clean water. Some people have suggested that this treatment is unsanitary, so ask questions before you indulge. There have been concerns about the use of the same fish on every patron, fearing that they may carry disease from the last person. It has not been proven yet; however, anything can happen.

In China, the fish pedicure treatment fee is 44,000 Yuan (about $6,800) for a deluxe luxury treatment.

KAYA SPA + STUDIO: TRIBE HOTEL, NAIROBI, KENYA

The Kaya Spa + Studio is located in the five-star Tribe Hotel in Nairobi, Kenya. *Conde Nast Traveler* voted this hotel and the spa as one of the best in Africa. The Rasul Chamber is a luxurious treatment the spa offers. The treatment is set in the African traditional Rasul Steam Chamber where your body is smeared with rich mineral mud onto the skin. The chamber warms up with a eucalyptus infused steam to soften the mud and relax the senses.

The ritual is completed with a soft, warm tropical rain shower that removes the mud and leaves the skin silky smooth. The Rasul Chamber treatment combines the four elements of water, fire, earth, and air into a unique and decadent spa experience. The cost: 2,000 shillings per person for 25 minutes.

EXHALE DAY SPA: WESTIN HOTEL AND RESORT, ST. MARTEEN

While in St. Marteen (on the Dutch side) I visited Exhale Day Spa and indulged in some of the spa's premier treatments while on vacation. My treatments consisted of a one-hour massage and body exfoliation sea salt scrub. The results were amazing! I was left feeling soft, silky, and relaxed. I followed up with fifteen minutes in the steam room. Steaming is very good for your skin. It opens pores and releases toxins through sweating. It was so good that I went to have a massage every day for the duration of my vacation while in St. Marteen.

EXHALE DAY SPA: WESTIN HOTEL AND RESORT, DOMINCIAN REPUBLIC

The Westin Resort Hotel and Spa, Exhale Day Spa is one of my favorite spas on the planet. My personal favorite is the Vitamin body wrap. A mixture of moisturizer containing vitamins and minerals are massaged onto the body and then it is wrapped in a foil that slightly heats up for twenty minutes. Once you're done, a streaming downpour of water from a Vichy shower washes the mixture away and a body polish is applied to keep the skin ultra-radiant and smooth.

Courtney Rashon

THE FERN TREE SPA: HALF MOON RESORT: MONTEGO BAY, JAMACIA

Nestled at the super exclusive Half Moon Resort, the Fern Tree Spa is tropical. Warm coconut and exotic fruit trees are located on the property. When I visited, the coconut milk and honey wrap was the treatment of choice, accompanied by a traditional Swedish massage. My body was left feeling smooth, silky, hydrated, and refreshed. The 50-minute treatment included coconut oils and honey slathered all over my body and I wrapped in plastic, while the body conditioner soaked into my skin. A Vichy shower was given to remove the product, followed by a Swedish massage to release tension.

BLISS SPA: W HOTEL, HOBOKEN, NEW JERSEY

The body buff exfoliating treatment is a combination of sea salt and lime, known as the Elemis Exotic lime and ginger salt body scrub. This signature treatment starts with a light exfoliation all over the body using a soft brush. After the exfoliation, I rinsed off and warm Japanese camellia oil was placed all over my body. My skin was left glowing and smooth and smelled delicious. This treatment is approximately 60 minutes.

ARMONIA SPA: HOTEL PUEBLO BONITO PACIFICA GOLF RESORT AND SPA: CABO SAN LUCAS, MEXICO

This spa is nestled in a beautiful, holistic, Zen and Feng Shui inspired hotel, which provides an extremely relaxing environment, complete with minimalistic décor and an abundance of tranquility. This happens to be my hotel of choice when visiting Cabo San Lucas.

I enjoyed an 80-minute detoxifying body wrap treatment, where the technician used exotic blends of honey and grains as a scrub to rid my skin of dull, dry skin cells.

Afterwards, a detoxifying blend of emollients and seaweed was applied to my body to release my toxins, and I was wrapped in a cocoon (or burrito) like large foil wrap while the concoction seeped into my pores and nourished my skin.

After the Vichy shower, I ended with a Swedish oil massage to relax my muscles and keep my skin moisturized. All three steps in this procedure were well worth the price.

BLUE MERCURY SPA: TROPICANA HOTEL, ATLANTIC CITY, NEW JERSEY

Blue Mercury Spa is a full-service spa known for both housing many cosmetic brands and providing a variety of decadent treatments. During my visit there, I was able to have the pleasure of experiencing the Classic Blissful Coconut Sugar Scrub. Not only is pure, unrefined coconut amazing for the skin, but it also leaves a delicious smell lingering for hours.

The treatment starts off with a blend of organic sugar, virgin cold-pressed coconut oil, and nut extractions. This luxurious blend of ingredients is used to exfoliate and get rid of dry, flaky skin.

Afterwards, a body massage is administered using a milk protein cream, enriched with Vitamins A, C, and E. My skin was super soft and silky, like a newborn baby. The indulgence lasts for 50 minutes, and I cannot wait to return to experience this again!

SPA TOCCARE: BORGOTA HOTEL CASINO AND SPA, ATLANTIC CITY, NEW JERSEY

This spa is located in the Borgota Hotel Casino and Spa, and the treatments were difficult to choose from. I decided to start with a Swedish massage that lasted for an hour and followed up with a deep-sea renewal scrub. And yes, this girl loves her body scrubs. It is a great way to rid the skin of dry, flaky, dead skin and expose new, fresh, and softer skin after the application.

First, my entire body was exfoliated with a Yuzu Sugar scrub. Using ginger and sea kelp to create a mask to hydrate the skin, my body was completely wrapped up like a mummy. During this time, I received a eucalyptus and lavender foot massage that was to die for! Afterwards, my entire body was moisturized from head to toe, leaving me feeling relaxed, detoxified, and extremely hydrated.

GRAND SPA AT MGM GRAND: MGM GRAND/ SIGNATURE HOTEL, LAS VEGAS, NEVADA

Located on the Las Vegas strip, the MGM Grand hotel has many other features besides gambling. The luxe hotel bears a boutique section known as the Signature Hotel with a fully stocked spa and a variety of treatments. I was in beauty heaven with all the products that were at my disposal. My treatments included a heated stone massage, where hot stones are placed down the center of your back to target pressure points. Afterwards, I experienced a sea salt body scrub, which I love, then relaxing and renewal time in the steam room.

SPA CASTLE NEW YORK: COLLEGE POINT, NY

The enormous Spa Castle was a dream. I felt like a princess in a fairytale when I saw the huge castle-inspired spa. There were many different options to choose from in terms of treatments. I was there with my best girlfriend, celebrating her bachelorette party.

Since that was the case, I had to be modest, due to the scheduling of girl fun and activities. However, I took full advantage of the general admission fee that allowed us to utilize every available free experience, excluding massages and treatments.

My favorite freebie, so to speak, which was included in the admission, was the Serenity pool. The pool was infused with vitamin and minerals that promised detoxification. My girlfriends and I luxuriated in this pool until the evening, and experienced a rock and crystal sauna that was relaxing, and a steam room designed to hydrate and breathe.

THE SPA AT DORAL FORRESTIAL: DORAL FORRESTAL HOTEL, PRINCETON FORESSTAL VILLAGE, PRINCETON, NEW JERSEY

Body wrap, Vichy shower, mineral bath, and sea salt glow is a day of total relaxation. Each year, I make it a tradition to visit this spa located in the Marriott Hotel (formally Doral Forrestal Hotel) and Conference Center with my mother and grandmother during Mother's Day.

We treat ourselves to a variety of treatments, enjoy a Spa lunch, and relax and detox in the steam room and sauna— not to mention purchase our favorite skincare products by Dermalogica and SkinCeuticals.

The mineral bath happened to be my all-time favorite treatment. Warm water is placed in a tub filled with jets to massage your back and body, and eucalyptus, seaweed, and minerals are immersed into the water to create a feeling of being in a natural hot spring. The massage therapist gently massaged my temples, scalp, and shoulders while my body was being rid of all the toxins.

Afterwards, I was whisked off to a treatment room where I received a 25-minute salt glow scrub and a 60-minute massage, followed up by one of my favorite moisturizers on the market. I can honestly say that this has been one of my best spa experiences right here at home, in the USA.

ELIZABETH ARDEN RED DOOR SPA: NEW YORK, NEW YORK

Fabulous, historic, classy, and luxurious is how I would describe the famed Red Door Spa. This was my first experience at the lavish spa. The only way I can describe it: breathtaking! The Swedish massage alone was worthy of bragging rights. All women should experience Elizabeth Arden Red Door Spa at least once in their lifetime. Classic!

Note: For more around the world beauty treatments visit my website @courtneyrashon.me

THINGS THAT ARE TACKY WHILE AT THE SPA

- Unkept feet (unless you are getting a pedicure)
- Stealing (robes, pillows, towels, footwear, paper goods, or community toiletries for everyone to use)
- Urinating in the public Jacuzzi or swimming pool
- Not flushing the toilet after use. It's just plain gross and unladylike. Also, do not, under any circumstances, flush tampons or sanitary napkins down the toilet.
- Gawking and staring at another patron's body. It's rude, and if she's comfortable being naked in the steam room or sauna, so be it. So, just relax and close your eyes or turn your head or come back later. (Do not feel insecure or weird because she is a perfect size or not!) Love the skin you're in!
- Loud and offensive language or behavior. This is a time to relax! WOOSAH! This is not a pep rally, a sporting event, or a cheerleading competition!

CHAPTER 15: WORLD'S MOST EXPENSIVE PRESENTS: THE GLAMOROUS LIFE

These particular spas, treatments, and products have received rave reviews and are extremely pricy. Most of us could buy a new car, put a down payment on condominium, or pay college tuition. These ultra luxurious treatments are afforded by the "rich and famous," or celebrities. But I have to give them an honorable mention and describe some of the most amazing and decadent hair, beauty products, and treatments that one could only imagine owning or experiencing!

FOOT FETISH

THE QUEEN OF FEET: MARGARET DABBS, SOLE SPA, LONDON, ENGLAND

Chiropodist Margaret Dabbs is synonymous with papering the feet of socialites and celebrities. Dubbed the "Queen Of Feet," she has been in the business of high-end pedicure spa treatments for many years. Her salon, Sole Spa London, is nestled in an exclusive secluded location in London where she likes to maintain her privacy, especially for her A-list clientele. The invigorating four-stage pedicure process she performs takes up to an hour or more, depending on the treatment.

Dabbs believes that your feet should never soak before removing dead skin and callous. She is known to use a special file made from crushed crystal, which removes dead skin and calluses instantly. Feet are then soaked, massaged, and slathered with her signature foot cream infused with vitamin A and D. Her salon also offers a wide range of services, including reflexology, and her renowned medical pedicure performed by podiatrists, which guarantees long lasting results. These treatments retail up to $2500.00, depending on the service.

Featured in *Conde Nast Traveler* as an extremely highly recommended salon in London, Dabbs has a line of products tailored just for feet. Her product line includes her hydrating foot soak, intensive foot oil, and an intense, hydrating foot lotion, as well as her one-of-a-kind crushed crystal file and the award-winning exfoliant foot mousse. All of her signature products are available for purchase online and sold at Bloomingdales stores in the U.S. and Space.NK. London. The products retail from $30 to $100.

<u>MANIS & PEDIS</u>

Nail beds are commanding an expensive price tag, depending on your taste level. Many ordinary polishes can look amazing without costing a fortune. But for celebrities and the super wealthy, the average polish can be deemed as being boring. Cosmetic companies have found a way to put a new spin on that everyday polish by infusing precious metals and gems and creating luxurious nail lacquers that now inflate the price of a mani and pedi.

Azature Black Diamond nail polish, also known as Black Diamond King, is one of the most expensive polishes in the world. Retailing at $250,000, this ultra decadent lacquer contains 367 carats worth of black diamonds and was created by Azature, the jewelry couturier.

Gold Rush Couture nail polish by Models Own is a rich gold lacquer that shines like diamonds on a bed of gold. The lid is proudly made of solid gold and encrusted with 1118 white diamonds. This polish retails for $130,000.

Iced manicures are beautiful and leave your nails sparkling. Ten carats of diamonds are applied to the fingertips in a traditional "French manicure," and can cost up to $51,000.

I Do by Ellie Cosmetics has a nail lacquer that is platinum-power-infused with creamy lacquer. The bottle is 100 percent pure platinum and was launched in Las Vegas in 2005. The product retails for $55,000 per bottle.

Red Carpet Manicure is the least expensive on the list. For $1000, this gel polish with LED formula consists of four carats worth of diamonds. The black-diamond-infused formula leaves nails shimmering and gorgeous.

BEAUTIFUL BATHS

EVIAN BATHS: HOTEL VICTOR, SOUTH BEACH, MIAMI FLORIDA

Hotel Victor is located in the posh section of Florida known as South Beach. This hotel's spa, Spa V, offers an exclusive bath known as the Evian Water bath. Not only does this water taste great and provides hydration for the body, but it purifies the senses and revitalizes the skin.

To quench your body's thirst, the bath requires 1000 one-liter bottles of the popular and expensive French mineral water. A 350-gallon infinity tub is then filled with Evian water. This luxurious spa treatment is priced at $11,000. As a guest at the hotel, the treatment will be discounted at $5000, providing the $6000-a-night suite is rented.

The hotel also has a special edition variation of the bath using only Christian La Roux Evian water, which is said to keep the skin supple because of the delicate water, which serves as a detoxification for the body. This treatment carries a price tag of $13,000. Celebrities like Serena Williams have indulged in this pricey but glamorous bath.

ME! BATHS TREATMENTS

ME! Baths has created a luxurious and majestic bath experience. Also known as the "eighth continent," this lavish bath is not your traditional bubble bath. Loaded with rare oils and exotic ingredients, it guarantees to leave your skin supple and silky. The bath waters consist of Hawaiian deep-sea water combined with glacier waters for a refreshing soak. Peruvian pink salts, and one-of-a-kind Arabian Sidr honey along with 24-carat gold shavings are added into the bath waters as well to create an opulent sophistication and distinct glow. Jojoba oils from Israel, Kokum butter from India, Murmuring butters from the Amazon, and Illipe butter from Borneo are infused for soothing, hydrating, conditioning and moisturizing.

Upon purchase, the treatment arrives in a beautiful, handcrafted, sterling silver, diamond-encrusted case. The case is exquisitely crafted and constructed in Israel. ME! Baths can be brought exclusively to your home. This indulgence is also available at select hotel spas around the world, such as the Ritz-Carlton. The cost for the self-indulgent luxury treatment generally retails for $50,000.

Me! Baths is known as one of the most expensive bath treatments in the world.

GEMSTONE FACIALS

Diamonds are forever and truly every woman's best friend. The same can be said about many precious gemstones that can adorn our necks, fingers, earlobes, and wrists. But what about being infused into a facial or body cream? This trend has become popular with many cosmetic companies, high-end salons, and spas, and can command a hefty price tag.

Many high-end salons or medical spas are participating in this ultra fabulous beauty trend, which seems to have celebrities flocking to their favorite spas and indulging in this luxurious treatment. There are various precious gemstones that are being used to create luminous, flawless, and glowing skin.

White Diamond Cream facials are the most popular facial in posh salons. This treatment incorporates micronized diamonds (ground up very fine) and quartz crystals into a hydrating cream. It provides skin with a healthy natural glow, as well as softness. The micronized diamonds also act as an exfoliant, which removes dead skin cells and allows new skin to become visible with less wrinkles and a radiant sheen. This procedure can cost between $1000 and $4000.

Black Diamond Cream facials are the newest and most trending facial to date. Unlike their counterparts, white diamonds, black diamonds are loaded with carbonado, which instantly absorbs and manipulates invisible UV light. The black diamonds are incorporated into a facial cream, infusing peptides that leave the skin with the appearance of being "airbrushed." Fine lines and wrinkles are diffused, and microcirculation stimulates the delivery of fresh blood to the tiny blood vessels in the face. This targets the base of the skin's epidermis and evens out skin tone while providing an amazing shimmer and vibrant glow. This procedure can cost between $2000 and $5000.

Pearl Cream facials consist of pearl powder that is rich in amino acids, calcium, sugars, and peptides that stimulate cell renewal and help fight glucagon (which is skin damage caused by sugars). This procedure fights pigmentation and enhances the natural radiance of the skin. The procedure can cost $1000 and up.

<u>FACE OFF</u>

BEE VENOM FACIALS: AESTHETICS OF LONDON, LONDON, ENGLAND

Bee Venom facials are a British-based treatment available at the Aesthetics of London. The Bee Venom regeneration facial consists of bee venom being placed on your face to plump the skin by tricking it into believing that it has been stung.

The skin-enhancing treatment promises to rejuvenate the skin, reduce the appearance of scars, fine lines, and wrinkles, and heals acne in the face by stimulating the production of collagen and elastin. Genius! The price tag for this bee sting can cost up to $55,200 per ounce of bee venom, or £300 per session.

VAMPIRE FACIALS

A visit to the day spa can be a scene from your favorite horror movie. The latest trend in liquid fillers that has estheticians outfitting celebrity clients is known as the **Vampire facial** or **Vampire facelift**.

The treatment was developed by the company Selphyl and costs $1,500 and up, depending on the procedure and location. This technique requires blood to be drawn from the patient's arm with a needle and then combined with restylane or juviderm and injected back into the client's face. OUCH!

The outcome? The facial produces and stimulates collagen production, which creates new skin, and removes fine lines and acne scars. The procedure takes about 45 minutes to an hour. The effects are not permanent and can last for a few months. The patient then has to return for new injections to keep up the maintenance.

BODY LANGUAGE
RUBY & DIAMOND EXFOLIATION BODY TREATMENT

Exquisite gems that include rubies and diamonds are being grinded into a super fine powder and used as an exfoliation treatment for the skin. There is a slight discomfort, but like the saying goes, "no pain, no gain." An ice cube is given to patrons to suck on to reduce swelling. The treatment was created by Scott-Vincent Borba and costs a whopping $7,000 per session.

GADGETS

Dutch Jewelry designer Ted Norton has cleverly revolutionized a new way of carrying makeup. Instead of the traditional makeup bag, Norton has created a device known as a cosmetic firearm. Designed to resemble an actual gun, this gadget comes complete with a variety of items needed to ensure beauty and glamour, as well as carrying every day essentials. The luxury glam gun retails between $11,500 to $17,000, and is handcrafted with 18-carat gold accents and components. The cosmetic firearm contains a choice of Dior or Chanel lipstick, antique hairpin, 18-carat gold toothpick, a vial of perfume, a 50-gram, 24-carat gold bar, USB stick, and a Viagra pill. The unique device can be found online and is a one-of-a-kind staple piece in any woman's accessory collection.

This innovative way to store makeup is not only trendy and chic, but also edgy. The contents are included with every purchase. In any given situation, the gun is equipped with everything any woman could possibly need. Also, the gun can be refilled with its original products and can store personal items as well. The cosmetic firearm is available on the web, but quantities are limited.

The cosmetic firearm is available in Dior 001 white, with an asking price of $11,500, and pays homage to the luxury brand Christian Dior. The cosmetic firearm is also available in the classic black Chanel 001 and has similar accessories, retailing slightly higher at $17,000 due to the exclusivity of the brand. Both guns are refillable with the original items they were equipped with upon purchase. Accessories such as special holsters and carrying cases are also available for purchase as well.

Gold and diamonds are not just adorning your body these days; they are also being made for your eyes. Gold and diamond-encrusted contact lenses are an elaborate, expensive, and new way to bejewel your eyes. Custom made, gold-plated lenses, featuring 18 glittering diamonds are the latest trend in contact lens eyewear.

The blinged out contact lens eyewear is a new custom jewelry line created by ophthalmologist Chandrasekhar Chawn of the Indian Research Center, Shekhar Eye Research. The doctor professes that the eyewear is very safe to wear and poses no risk of damaging the cornea, despite the negative media attention it received. Chandra Boston scleral lenses are used to create the bejeweled lenses. This particular brand of contact lens is generally used to treat eye illness. The contact lenses weigh about five grams in total and sit between 6 mm and 9 mm away from the cornea. The jewelry part of the lens does not touch the cornea at all.

The inspiration behind the creation was Dr. Chandrasekhar Chawn's wife who had diamonds put into her teeth. He hopes that Bollywood actors wanting to create a new and exciting look will use the product. The cost of such lavish eye jewelry is $15,000 a pair. A limited edition of 4,000 pairs will be created and sold exclusively through Shekhar Eye Research.

LUXURY LOCKS

Anyone can have long, lavish locks by adding hair extensions. Different colors, textures, and lengths can be achieved due to the variety of extensions that are out on the market today. There are also many techniques that are used to achieve this look. Glued extensions, sewn-in extensions, and bonded and fusion extensions are just a few ways hair can be added to your own natural hair to create the desired style. The cost of this procedure can vary depending on the type of hair used and the application process.

To date, the most expensive extensions retail at $10,000. Gemini14 salon in New York, located in West Village, offers this elaborate service. Two hundred and fifty thousand strands or more of human hair are applied to the natural hair by using a bonding system. This can take up to nine hours. Each strand or strands are applied at the root and bonded using a hot plier tool. The keratin protein polymer bond used to adhere the extensions allows them to last longer, cause less damage, and look completely natural.

The hair used is special in and of itself. Virgin hair donated by Indian women to Hindu temples as part of a religious offering is used to make the extensions. The strands are de-pigmented using a special "osmosis" process and are untouched by chemicals. The hair can be dyed, cut, colored, and styled in any fashion. The "touch up" method is basically having the bond tightened when "new growth" appears using the plier tool. This can cost $2,000 or more, and should be done every four to six weeks.

Many celebrities are huge fans of the salon's extensions and are willing to pay the hefty price tag. Many women are flocking to this salon to get the perfect extensions. There is a waiting list for up to two weeks at the posh salon.

Harrods luxury department store located in London houses the luxury Urban Retreat beauty mecca. There are a variety of services offered to keep anyone looking their best. The blow-dry treatment available at the super plush salon is rumored to leave your hair gorgeous and healthy. The blow-dry treatment is priced at $500 or £320.

This treatment is dubbed as the most expensive blow-dry treatment across the world. Made with diamond dust and meteorite extracts, the blow-dry treatment guarantees the hair will be left shiny and silky. The one-of-a-kind treatment was created with luxurious and expensive ingredients. The diamond dust is made from pure diamonds and was added to strengthen the hair. The meteors are obtained from the Sea of Japan where they react to seawater and produce rich botanicals and minerals that are excellent for maintaining beautiful locks.

First, the hair is shampooed with Truffle by Fuente UK, a shampoo infused with diamonds and meteorites with white truffle skin. Afterwards, the conditioner containing the same ingredients is applied. The conditioner is rinsed out, and the hair is coated with the enriched treatment and blown out directly into the hair. The blow-dry treatment penetrates and rejuvenates the hair shaft, leaving it strong and manageable. Also, a complimentary, full-size bottle of both the shampoo and conditioner is given to each client to take home. The blow-dry treatment is one of Urban Retreat's most popular requests.

__MAKEUP MADNESS__

H. Couture beauty mascara is the world's most expensive mascara. The creator of this luxury mascara is Tasha Smith Valez, who established the brand in 2006. The product provides lashes with amazing volume, as well as lash conditioning and extensive length when applied.

The casing is adorned with 1000 Swarovski crystals, which beef up the price tag. The casing was upgraded when a celebrity client requested a mascara casing to be made of 18-carat gold with 2,500 blue diamonds. It retailed at $14 million.

This amazing mascara includes lifetime refills, a private concierge service, 24/7-phone support as well as discounts and gift-wrapping services.

Eyelashes are now getting all dressed up. The traditional eyelash strip has gotten a stylist and has become more unique and lavish. Krē•āt, established in 2009 by Taylor Chang Babaian, is responsible for this upgrade. Gold and diamond lashes, which are listed on the company's website, have been a popular trend on the red carpet and in major fashion magazines. In 2011, the company began to manufacture these beautiful jeweled false eyelashes and made them exclusively for Barneys, NYC.

These luxurious eyelashes are made with human hair and are customized according to the client's desired length. Each set of eyelashes is embellished with tiny white diamonds and 18-carat gold. Every eyelash strip is adorned with the precious stones and decadent gold to create a look that truly reflects wealth and luxury. The application takes about one hour to apply, retails for $1,350 dollars and are made to order.

Guerlain's KissKiss Gold and Diamonds has been labeled as the World's most expensive lipstick. The super-rich lip color was created in France and became obtainable to the

United States in November 2007. This high-end exquisite lipstick is known for its staying power when applied and offers elasticity and suppleness to the lips due to natural high quality ingredients such as Vitamin E and Vitamin A for conditioning.

What makes this lipstick so expensive? The super luxury product is encased in an 18-carat solid gold tube and is embellished with 199 sparkling pavé diamonds. The high precision lipstick is available in 15 custom shades and comes with its very own lip brush and a velvet case. The gold encasing can also be engraved and the lipstick is refillable. The prestigious lip color is also housed in a black lacquered wooden case.

The designer Herve Van Der Straeten teamed up with Guerlain to give the consumer something extraordinary and fabulous. The brand is known for its innovative cosmetics and luxury high end products. The price for such a small piece of luxury is $62,000 and can be purchased at Guerlain boutiques around the world.

TOP FIVE FACIAL TREATMENTS

After plenty of research, the results are in. The editors of various fashion magazines, spas, estheticians, makeup artists, cosmetic companies, and women and men across the country have voted. Here are the top five facials (in no particular order) and the benefits they provide.

Gold Facials. This technique provides skin whitening and contains anti-aging components. Gold dust, gold powder, and gold foil are melted with heat and applied to the skin.

Pearl Facials. This procedure leaves skin naturally glowing. Pearl powder contains amino acids and calcium, which help fight pigmentation and discoloration of the skin. It also rejuvenates the skin's appearance and promotes cell renewal.

Fruit Facials. This works best for oily skin and is also great for exfoliation. This technique keeps the skin supple and usually contains herbal infusions as well as fruit such as pineapple, papaya, and strawberry. It keeps the skin hydrated and full of moisture.

Diamonds. This decadent facial removes dead skin cells and acts as an exfoliant as well. Diamond powder removes the appearance of fine lines and wrinkles, leaving the skin with a natural, healthy glow.

Wine. This unique facial is for normal skin. It removes tans and hydrates the skin, leaving it rejuvenated and supple. It can also leave you feeling "buzzed" if you happen to have more than a few sips.

CHAPTER 16: WHAT A GIRL NEEDS

Moisturizing warm baths, bath salts, and exfoliation are all key to maintaining healthy skin with a healthy glow. Of course, proper diet, exercise, and sleep will aid in keeping a healthy you. The following are my top ten beauty products I feel everyone should have to keep it going.

10 ESSENTIAL BEAUTY PRODUCTS

1. Sunscreen: Protects the skin from the sun's UV rays.
2. Glycolic Acid: Gets rid of hyper-pigmentation—a.k.a. dark spots and discoloration.
3. Face and Body exfoliants: By exfoliating, you rid your body of dead skin on the surface.
4. Ingrown hair treatment pads: Gets rid of razor or hair bumps "downtown."
5. Mineral foundation: It is lightweight and helps to avoid a shiny face.
6. Hydrating hair oils and moisturizing masks for the hair: They coat the hair and strengthen the hair shaft.
7. Balm: Good old fashion petroleum jelly does the trick! This is great for knees and elbows.
8. Foundation: Foundation is perfect for maximum coverage. Tinted moisturizer is lightweight, and can be used as a substitute for foundation but provides less coverage.
9. Co-wash and scalp soothers: These shampoos will prevent itching and inflammation and calm your irritated scalp.

10. Moisturizer: It keeps your skin soft and hydrated.

TRICKS & TIPS

I just had to share this tidbit of information. I swear by this product! Mario Badescu Pink Drying Lotion eliminates pimples instantly. The solution contains camphor, sulfur, salicylic acid, and calamine.

Cleanse first, tone, and moisturize, then apply the lotion with a cotton swab directly on the spot. The drying lotion dries quickly and eliminates whiteheads overnight and can be used for back acne and breakouts on the chest. It can also soothe the itch from mosquito bites. It's also safe for all skin types. Make sure the bottle is on a flat surface with the pink sediment resting on the bottom. Use daily until the pimples are gone. The pink lotion is available online or in Ulta beauty and Sephora stores.

For dry, irritated, and itchy skin due to eczema, I would recommend using Aveeno Oatmeal treatments. This soothing treatment will calm irritated skin and provide immediate relief. In a warm bath, pour a packet of the treatment into the bath water and soak. The oatmeal dissolves into the warm water, which causes the water to become cloudy. I use two packets for maximum results. After soaking in the bath for fifteen minutes, apply a thick and heavy moisturizer such as Eucerin lotion for dry skin, or Gold Bond medicated lotion for eczema.

Raw and pure unrefined African Shea butter is another moisturizer that is amazing for all skin types. Raw, untreated African Shea butter is very thick and usually yellow in color. African Shea butter is a natural product that works well for keeping the skin smooth, reducing the appearance of cellulite, dark spots, skin discolorations, wrinkles, and blemishes. It is also an outstanding moisturizer that will keep your skin soft and healthy because of the therapeutic properties. The product is heavy and goes on thick, so be sure to make sure that once the product is in your hands, to rub the butter until it become softer and creamy in texture. Then apply it directly to your skin. The results are incredible.

African Shea butter is made from the nut of the African Shea tree. This type of butter is high in fatty acid and contains vitamins E and F, which is are essential for moisturizing and rejuvenating the skin.

For reducing inches around the middle, I use a product that comes from Colombia, which is called Gel Sauna Eucalipto. This product can be found online or in a predominately Latin populated area at a beauty supply store. The cream is mentholated and contains eucalyptus. I apply the cream around my midsection and wrap it with clear plastic wrap from underneath my breast all the way down to my waist and leave it on for about 20 to 40 minutes. For maximum results, I sometimes use a waist trainer or wear a corset to assist in this process.

Now, I know this sounds weird and uncomfortable, but I can honestly say that after doing this procedure twice a week for a few months, it works and is less painful and less expensive than cosmetic surgery. I will even hit the gym wearing this ensemble for more results. Try it!

CHAPTER 17: GRANDMA'S KITCHEN

Beauty treatments, creams, lotions, and potions can be expensive. There are many natural home remedies that you can find right in your kitchen cabinets and refrigerators. Here are a few ways to beat the costs and keep your hair, skin, and nails fabulous with simple home remedies:

Oatmeal is not just for breakfast anymore. Oatmeal is great as a soothing and anti-inflammatory substance. It contains beta-glucans, which is a soluble fiber that creates a thin film on the surface of your skin. For an oatmeal skin treatment, place a handful of oatmeal in a washcloth and secure it with a rubber band and soak it in warm water. Squeeze the cloth into the water; once the water becomes cloudy, splash it on your face and then air-dry or pat your face gently with a cloth.

Eggs contain high amounts of protein and are beneficial as a hair conditioner. Combine eggs and two tablespoons of olive oil to your dry hair. Wrap hair with a hot towel for 10 minutes. Afterwards shampoo, work up a lather, rinse, and condition. This helps the hair retain luster and resilience.

Oranges slough off dead skin and the acid contained in the juicy fruit loosens dead skin cells. Cut an orange in half and rub the orange on your elbows, heels, knees, and any other dry spots in your body.

Got Milk? People have been using milk for baths for centuries. The lactic acid in milk gently exfoliates the skin,while the milk fat serves as a body moisturizer. Add a gallon of milk to your bath water and soak.

Apple Cider Vinegar has many health benefits. Believe it or not, apple cider vinegar can help to protect your skin from blemishes caused by bacteria. Combine apple cider vinegar and boiled parsley water with four to five drops of tea tree oil as an antiseptic and pour into a spray bottle. Parsley is a skin-clarifying herb. Shake well and spray your face. Refrigerate the rest after use.

Lemons, Lemons, Lemons. Lemons are a natural skin brightener. The acid in lemons will fade discolorations on the body. Simply cut a lemon in half and apply it directly onto clean skin. Repeat this daily, and the discoloration will start to fade away. Also, lemon water is also a surefire way to brighten your skin. Cut a piece of lemon and drop it in your favorite bottled water or squeeze the juice into the water, which I find to be more effective. Drink lemon water every day and you will see results within two weeks.

Coo-Coo for Coconuts. Pure virgin unprocessed, raw coconut oil is an excellent product for hair, skin, and nails. Coconut oil contains essential oils that are powerful agents for moisturizing and keeps everything healthy and hydrated. Make sure the coconut oil is unbleached and has not been hydrogenated or refined in any way.

The many functions that coconut oil can provide are astonishing! It works well for removing eye makeup, but you still have to wash your face afterwards. Coconut oil can be used as a hair conditioner. Apply coconut oil to clean damp hair. Leave it in for ten minutes, and for a deeper conditioning treatment, a plastic cap or shower cap can be worn for maximum hydration. Rinse your hair thoroughly and style as usual. Coconut oil strengthens weak hair, and moisturizes frizzy and dry hair as well. As a body moisturizer, apply the product all over your body to keep your skin soft. It can also be used to keep your cuticles intact. Use it in solid form or as a liquid. Just pop a generous amount into the microwave and heat for thirty seconds.

Tea Time. Tea bags can reduce the swelling and puffiness from underneath your eyes. Apply warm tea bags underneath your eyes to draw out inflammation and soothe tired eyes.

Cool Cucumbers. Cucumbers are great in salads and even better for revitalizing eyes. Slice a cucumber into circles and soak them in warm water. Close your eyes and apply the cucumbers directly to your eyelids. Leave them on for ten minutes or so. This will leave your eyes refreshed and calm.

Soda Pop Baking soda has many uses. This "oldie but goodie" substance can be used to keep teeth bright and white. Dip your wet toothbrush in baking soda and brush. Baking soda does not contain fluoride, so make sure you use toothpaste with fluoride as well.

Baking soda can also be used as a solution to soothe sensitive skin post-shave. Combine one teaspoon of baking soda with a cup of warm water to create a soothing solution. Simply rub it on your legs to instantly remedy razor burn.

Baking soda can also be used as deodorant, but make sure it doesn't get clumpy or cakey underneath your armpits. Just mix it with water to create a paste with a consistency that isn't too watery or runny. For added comfort and a better wetness protection, add a tablespoon of cornstarch.

CHAPTER 18: HIM

We all have a HIM. And even if you don't, there will eventually be a HIM. HIM is dedicated to all the husbands, boyfriends, partners, brothers, best friends, homies, lovers, and friends.

Just like women, men should be groomed as well. Being well-groomed and conscious of hygiene should be part of his daily regimen.

Manscaping is when the body hair is trimmed down so it appears manicured like a lush lawn. Manscaping can occur on any part of the body including chest, underarms, back, and pubic area. Not only can the hair smell, but it can be scratchy and irritating if you have sensitive skin. Men should also get manicures and pedicures. Crusty, ashy, and callused feet are not sexy on anyone, especially men. There are certain exceptions for hands, only because some men work with their hands, but please use lotion and get a manicure.

Sometimes, men believe that they are exempt from being well-groomed. Some men believe that being groomed is only for a woman. The stigma of being "too feminine" associated with grooming is ancient history. Some men take grooming just as seriously as we do! Some people refer to the term associated with a man being adamant about his grooming rituals as "metro sexual," but for me, it's just a man caring about and taking pride in his appearance.

Facials and exfoliation aren't just for women; men need facials too. Facials rejuvenate your complexion and get rid of dry dull skin. Moisturizing is a must! This will keep his skin smooth and soft.

Fresh breath, clean teeth and a healthy mouth are extremely important. No one wants to kiss a dirty mouth! Leftover residue from smoking cigars or cigarettes is gross! Brush your teeth and your tongue! There isn't any other way I can put it.

After being out and working all day, the man should shower. In fact, everyone should shower. But men have the tendency to have stronger body odors than most women, so a quick lather all over the body—including the anus and scrotum—is essential.

Regular haircuts and facial grooming, including waxing or threading a uni-brow, are also important. A 5 o'clock shadow can be super sexy, but it has to be neat and "shaped up" if that is the look he is going for. Hair that has grown down the neck, and unruly, wild, wolverine facial hair is okay sometimes, if you're into the grunge look, but less is more regarding facial hair.

THINGS THAT ARE TACKY

- Raggedy toupee
- Uni-brow
- Christmas wreath around the head (just shave it— why hold on to three strands?)
- Deodorant chips and residue stuck to underarm hairs
- Yellow and chipped teeth
- Dirty and ragged fingernails (in our minds, we are saying: "Don't touch me down below or anywhere else!")

- Long toenails
- Waxy ear gook
- Stray hairs in the nostrils
- Ashy skin . . . ashy anything, including elbows, hands, and knees
- Dry and chapped lips
- Overpowering cologne
- Fading skid marks or lint balls on underwear
- "Tight-y Whities" that aren't so white
- Sunglasses at night (random, but it's true—unless you're a celebrity)
- Sweaty balls
- Laziness
- Extra loud snoring (with my eyes closed, I would have thought I was listening to the sounds of wild bears)
- Excessive perspiring—a.k.a. sweaty as hell!
- Scuffed shoes
- Sloppy or un-groomed overall appearance
- High-water pants (when they aren't supposed to be) ill-fitting suit, overly baggy anything. Invest in a tailor.

THINGS WE LOVE

- Clean bed sheets (at his house)
- Boxer briefs/fitted tank tops
- 5 o'clock shadow (as long as it's neat and groomed)
- Crisp, white, tailored shirt
- Clear gloss on fingernails
- Sexy sideburns and goatee
- Bald heads

- Caesar or low haircuts
- Perfectly coifed, natural hair
- His facial and body products
- A tailored suit and a pair of designer shoes
- Nice teeth
- Exercising
- Smooth skin
- Cologne (but not too much)
- Toned arms and chest
- Nice ass in jeans

THINGS HE LOVES

- Lingerie (garters, crotch-less panties, push up bras, lace, fishnets, see-through or anything sheer, boy shorts, tank tops with or without a bra)
- Manicures
- Well-groomed eyebrows
- Red lipstick
- No makeup
- Ponytails
- Natural, wavy, beach hair
- Halle Berry haircuts
- Braids
- Glowing skin
- Exercising
- White teeth
- Black eyeliner
- Pedicures
- Glossy lips
- Sexy shoes
- A hint of perfume anywhere

- Eyeglasses

THINGS HE THINKS ARE TACKY

- Overly done, excessive makeup (are you auditioning for the local circus?)
- Overly exaggerated, fan-like, false, synthetic eyelashes
- Bad hair extensions
- Raggedy wig or hairpiece
- Chipped or missing nails (this applies to a manicure and pedicure)
- Fishy odor
- Too much perfume
- Greasy hair
- Ashy anything (this includes knees, elbows, and any other dry parts of the body). Moisturize!
- Hairy anything (moustache, pubic hair, underarm hair, uni-brow . . . wax, thread, get electrolysis, or shave if you must!)
- Big cotton undies that cover your navel
- Panty lines
- Crusty heels on feet, corns and bunions on toes
- Cheap shoes
- Mismatched bra and panties

FINAL THOUGHTS

Through my personal experiences and recommendations, I hope that you find this book helpful, entertaining, and informative. My mission is to educate and enhance the reader's relationship with makeup and provide some guidelines about which makeup applications would be the best, appropriate look for the occasion.

Making people beautiful and seeing the look on their faces once I have transformed them into an enhanced version of themselves is gratifying for me. Makeup is not a remedy for self-esteem or a prescription to feel better about yourself; it is a tool to enhance what beauty you already possess.

ABOUT THE AUTHOR

Beauty expert and celebrity makeup artist Courtney Rashon, is synonymous with all things creative. Known for her ability to transform the ordinary into something breathtaking, her abilities always exceed expectations. Not only does she possess the skills needed for everyday glamour makeup, she also excels as a special effects artist.

Ms. Rashon's career in makeup began while employed in the fashion industry as an executive assistant to the CEO of a high-end design company. Recognizing her passion for cosmetics, she began to explore the possibility of becoming a makeup artist.

After attending Cosmetology school in New York, she began working with a variety of artists, directors, industry personalities, and tastemakers, delivering the best looks for music videos, documentaries, photo shoots and special events. Courtney's company, Courtney Rashon Industries,

LLC, established in 2010, provides fashion and glamour makeup, visual effects makeup application, men's grooming, imaging, and mentoring for aspiring makeup artists.

Giving Face: The Art of Looking Flawless for Every Occasion is her first book.

Follow Courtney @:

Twitter: @courtneyrashon

Facebook: www.facebook.com/OfficialCourtneyRashon

Instagram: @courtney_rashon

Website: www.courtneyrashon.me

ACKNOWLEDGEMENTS & CREDITS

Cosby Media Publications

Leon Cosby III

Braxton Cosby

Ruth Morrison

What's the 411TV

Lawrence "Ben" Miles

New York Women's Chamber of Commerce (NYWCC)

NV Magazine

Kyle Donovan

PerchonokSmall

#PrettyGirlGangCosmetics™

Illustrator: Ariel Leopard

Photographer: Heather Hunter Photography

Makeup: Jacen Bowman

Public Relations: Heather West/ WestLevy PR

Legal: Drew Murray, ESQ.

ADDITIONAL CREDITS

All stories in the chapters titled "World's Most Expensive: The Glamorous Life" and "Around the World and Back" are written by Courtney Rashon, courtesy of Examiner.com